CUSTOM KICKS

KICKS

personalized footwear

Laurence King Publishing

contents

introduction

customizing is everywhere

Old cars are pimped into ghetto blasters on wheels, antique furniture gets a second chance in trendy stores, and even the Salvation Army has a project in which old clothing is turned into haute couture. Basically, everything can be customized. Customizing is modifying something to one's personal taste. It is particularly suitable for giving old stuff a new look, but it also gives the opportunity to personalize mass-produced stuff. With the world getting smaller every day, the urge to create your own unique identity grows.

a full circle

Totally handmade shoes are the *summum bonum* of customized shoes. Before the Industrial Revolution, all shoes were handmade. In many cultures, shoes represented one's social status. The poorest had nothing with which to cover their feet, while the upper classes covered them in the highest quality materials made by the best craftsmen in town. Some things have not changed: shoes are still a status symbol today. How they are made is what has changed. With the invention of the sewing machine it became

possible to make shoes more cheaply, so they became accessible to a wider audience. New inventions, materials and techniques followed quickly in the twentieth century to the point of mass production. Factories enable the production of many shoes at low cost. However, these shoes lack personality. This may be the reason we are seeing today a step back into the pre-industrialized era through customizing.

customized shoes are in

Customizing is a trend in fashion, but it booms in footwear. Customizing your own shoes is a way of stepping out of the crowd, of showing your identity. Sneakers were the first customized pairs, the progeny of urban culture and fashion. Proudly, Run DMC rapped about their 'Adidas' back in 1986. Customizing steadily gained popularity from the start of the new millennium. Customized shoes star in hip-hop videos, occupy forums on the Internet, and grace the catwalks. The trend started underground, on the streets where young people gather, but soon it also appeared in big customization parties. The crew behind Sneaker Pimps, for example, has a great

shoe art by Justin Lee Williams

shoe art by Sonni

shoe art by Cupco, www.cupco.net

following. Their parties bring art, fashion and music together. There are events on customized kicks all around the world. Celebrities – mostly people from the hip-hop world – proudly pay big bucks for their unique pair. There are many competitions worldwide and even a World Championship. In addition, many artists are now customizing shoes as a profession.

how it all started

Shoes have been a subject of artists for a long time, but now have become the canvas itself. Put a blank shoe and a marker in the hand of a creative person and magic is bound to happen. Blank shoes are perfect objects to handle. Spankin' new shoes, just out of the box, beg irresistibly to be painted on. The surfaces of most shoes can be treated with markers, spray-paint and other materials. The challenge lies in what to do with them. Do you want to change the colours and patterns of your favourite kicks and make all your friends jealous with your unique pair? Alternatively, do you treat this piece of three-dimensional canvas as you would a regular piece of canvas and wear your artwork on your

feet? The endless possibilities make customizing footwear something that anyone can do.

and the brands followed

Since showing personality became so popular, even the big brands have jumped in. Companies have found that individualized goods command a premium. First, they released shoes customized by artists in limited editions. Now there is the option of mass-customization. They use flexible computer-aided manufacturing systems to produce custom output. Those systems combine the low-unit costs of mass-production processes with the flexibility of individual customization.

For example, Vans provide the opportunity to customize slip-ons or old school sneakers with a choice of colours and patterns for the canvas. Similarly, Reebok has the RbkCustom line, where you can colour the whole shoe, from sole to stitchwork. Further, Converse offers the same with the Converse One line with options of customizing different types of Converse shoe. Finally, at NIKEiD you can choose width, outsole, colours and technical specs.

White shoes are typically the basis of

customization. Adidas created a line, Adicolor, which consists of white shoes that are sold with a variety of customization tools, ranging from magic markers and spray cans to lace jewels and interchangeable stripes. An Adicolor collection was first released in 1983, but it became a success when they rereleased it in 2006. Newcomer Tagür created a white shoe designed especially to be customized. Customizing is big and will only get bigger as brands extend customizing options. The fact that the big brands have joined the cause shows that this underground phenomenon has become increasingly popular and even mainstream.

about the book

This book shows a collection of personalized footwear: unique wearable art. Not only sneakers, but also high heels, flip-flops, roller skates and all kinds of shoe have been pimped. Footwear has been customized by artists from all over the globe, from all continents, of 30 nationalities and using many different styles and techniques. It is an interesting mixture of established designers and illustrators and upcoming talents. Some do this as a profession, while others are first-timers. Apart from the fact that unique shoes are awesome, customizing is real big fun. So get inspired and get started!

< *artwork by:*
top: Dave White, Tim Wolff, Logan Real
middle: Sekure D, Valero Doval, Josh Wisdumb
bottom: Eli Horn, Tangible Thoughts, Rist One

tips and advice

You can order a unique customized pair, or even let an artist customize your favourite shoes especially for you, but the high point of customizing would be personalizing your own shoes, if only because it's fun. The following tips might be useful. You don't want to ruin your favourite kicks...

first-timers

If it's your first time, it's recommended to try pimping old shoes first. Also, test the materials on the inside of the shoe, so you know what will happen. Invest in the right materials. If you want the shoes to be wearable, it's worth using high-quality material; otherwise paint will peel or crack, markers will fade in the sun, etc.

Be patient! Customizing takes a lot of time. Make sketches first, on a shoe template or with pencil on the shoe itself. Check which materials work on which kind of shoe surface. Canvas shoes might require different materials than leather sneakers.

But, on the other hand, you might just go nuts on a new pair of sneakers with whatever you can find and surprise yourself. If it's your first time and you don't have a steady hand yet, don't aim to create two identical shoes.

< *artwork by MAKI*

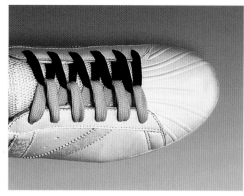

different styles and techniques

Customizing varies from changing the colour of the shoe and applying a pattern to creating complete illustrations on shoes. The options are unlimited.

• If you don't trust yourself with paint and brushes, laces are a great way of giving shoes a personal touch. You can buy many different kinds in stores and through the Internet: round, flat, coloured, striped, elastic, twisted, glittered or patterned. There are many different ways of tying the laces as well.

• Another way is decorating your shoes with stickers, buttons, beads, bling or whatever.

• Almost anything can be sewn on to (especially canvas) shoes. Pieces of cloth, labels, badges, socks, fur, etc. Do use strong needles though. And if you're no good with needles, try superglue.

• Iron-ons are also fun. This way you can get photos on your shoes. Make sure you check how long they will last.

• Markers are also quite easy to use. Buy high-quality permanent markers or paint markers and you can draw almost anything. They come in many colours, thick or thin, three-dimensional markers, glow-in-the-dark markers and many more. Markers are ideal to make detailed illustrations and lines. They also work well on non-canvas parts of the shoe like the rubber trim around the sole.

• By cutting you can create a whole different style or shape of shoe.

• And then of course there is paint. Paint requires some preparation and a lot of patience but can change a shoe completely. You can apply it with brushes and markers or spray-paint or airbrush it on to the surface. Paint is the easiest to use to colour big surfaces. There is a lot to choose from, as in colours, glossy or matt, metallic, sparkly, puffy, neon, etc.

• New techniques are used every day; one of them is lasering your shoes. This way you can cut out an illustration quite precisely.

And of course there are endless possible combinations!

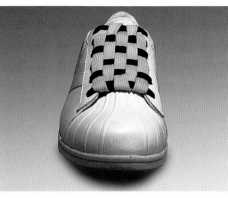

from a to z

An example of customizing a shoe from beginning to end:

- Get the shoes you want to customize, get inspired and make some sketches.
- Remove the laces from the shoes.
- Bundle some old rags and poke them inside to soak up any leaks and keep the shoe's shape.
- Use acetone or nail polish remover to strip the wax with cotton wool. It removes the coating and allows the paint to adhere better to the surface. It is available in local pharmacies or grocers. Since it is flammable and poisonous, use gloves and open a window.
- Sand the surface with fine sandpaper. Lazy people can use a drill but be careful not to go through the leather (unless you like holes).
- Clean the shoes with a wet towel or piece of cloth and let them dry.
- Tape any parts you don't want paint to go on. Also, cover your room if you don't like paint spots.
- Use acrylic paint to base paint the shoes. Again, open windows or do it outside.

- Add details, for example with markers or with a fine paintbrush. Use paint with a bigger brush or spray-paint for shapes. If you use spray-paint, stickers are ideal to use as stencils.
- Use many thin layers instead of one thick layer, and let each dry before starting another. If you create a new layer, use cellophane to cover up parts that don't need to be painted with the colour you're using at that moment. Tape or stickers will peel off paint that you have already applied...
- When the design is finished, apply a thin coat of clear acrylic spray. Let it dry, wait an hour and do it again. This will protect your creation. Again, get the right material; hairspray doesn't work.
- Put the laces back in.
- Wear your shoes with pride.

low budget tips

• Any shoe can be pimped into the most amazing one, so don't bother about buying expensive brands.

• Only work on the areas on the shoe that don't bend. This way the chance of paint cracking is smaller, so cheaper paint will do.

• When using cheaper paint, mix it with acetone. This makes the paint more flexible and less likely to crack.

• Markers are cheaper than paint.

• One or two different colours can make just as cool a design as four or five...

materials

Listed below are some materials used by artists in this book:

• (Permanent) Markers:
Sharpie markers
Letraset ProMarkers
Graffiti markers
Biro markers
Pilot V Razor Points
Faber-Castell brush markers
Posca pens
• Paint
Acrylic paints, such as Liquitex, Grumbacher, Delta Ceramics, Apple Barrel colours
Tempera paint
Magix
DecoArt SoSoft
QVC
Leather paint by Angelus
• Finish
Clear acrylic varnish spray
Gloss finish by Delta Ceramics
Matt finish by FolkArt (dull, non-reflective)
Minwax Gloss Polyurethane spray

C100 Studio
www.c100studio.com

Germany

I got these neon tapes, which are rare, at a lecture/workshop I held in Milan last year. The colour combination of neon pink and neon orange, together with black, goes really well. For months I wasn't sure in which project I was going to use the tape, until I stumbled on this old pair of Adidas Gazelle trainers. So customizing gave them a sort of rebirth.

Daniel Ting Chong
www.flickr.com/photos/softpencil

South Africa

The shoes entitled *Red Paint Spill Bill* were for an exhibition called 'Sneak' in Cape Town, South Africa. My style is quirky, simplistic and almost childlike. I have used spray-paints, inks, leather dyes, Kokis, Pantone pens and transfers. I don't really plan; I just get the shoe, research the materials and think of some sick colour combos and ideas.

21

Paul Rojanathara | PRART
www.prart.net

France

In my designs, I use sneakers as a support, like canvas for paintings. The artistic goal is to reveal the personality of the original shoes, to inject illustration into it or to change their colour or packaging material. The box is also a part of the sneaker. I want the original sneaker to be something unique, luxurious.

Emma Laiho

www.emmalaiho.net

Finland

These shoes must be my favourite shoes ever. I had worn them to shreds, but still couldn't bear to toss them. Turning them into a piece of art was a great way to say goodbye. As a mixed-media artist, I wanted to stretch the concept of customized shoes. I used Japanese origami paper. After a coat of varnish the surface is surprisingly durable and you can wear them (gently).

Warren Lewis & Senyol
www.worldwarwon.co.za

South Africa

I have customized many pairs of sneakers and organized a sneaker show in Cape Town entitled 'Sneak'. I work with mixed media like cotton, spray-paint, pens, matches, inks, etc. And I entitle my work using funny words. However, I have only once seen a pair of custom sneakers that I would wear. Shoes are shoes, after all.

Fall of the Phoenix: Sidual Apparel invited me to paint shoes for a raffle. I painted the Etnies to reflect Sidual's connection with the tattoo industry. The canvas-like Etnies were the perfect design and material for acrylic paint.

Eli Horn
www.outwardcreative.com

Canada

Aaron Hogg

www.moadesign.net

New Zealand

I wanted something to save me from the bleary-eyed confusion of figuring out which foot to put in which shoe in the morning. This is the solution. Initially, I intended to use a monotone black-line treatment. My wife suggested the gold and silver, which was a good call. My style for this piece is channelling Peter-Max-esque, with psychedelic flora, fauna and objects to weave patterns and contours.

IMAKETHINGS
www.imakethings.co.uk

UK

I bought these plimsolls from a charity shop and painted them with acrylics especially for this book. I tried to customize some Converse high-tops once before, but they were pretty rubbish so I was worried about how these would turn out. I'm actually quite happy with them. My girlfriend now wears them out and about, but only if it isn't raining.

Greg M. Washington
www.inqmnd.ca

Canada

Greg M. Washington uses bright colours and patterns. He also uses coloured laces that match the colours of the shoe.

André Trenier | Tangible Thoughts
www.tangiblethoughts.com

USA

The guys at Tangible Thoughts create custom sneaker designs and specialize in detailed illustrations. They mostly pimp Nikes.

My shoes are infected by a freaky pink character virus. The creatures live inside the virus and crawl out when shoes are in range. I used my old skate sneakers and spray-painted one in pink and the other one in green. This way it seems that the virus is still spreading.

Emiel Almoes
www.3wielr.com

The Netherlands

Christian Bielke | Johnny Jaywalker
www.johnnyjaywalker.blogspot.com

Norway

This is a shoe I did in response to an email request. It's a Nike Air Force 1 – originally completely white, now customized by me.

Josh Wisdumb
www.joshwisdumb.com

USA

I describe my 'style' of art as discombobulated faces in abstract places. When customizing anything, you are transforming one piece of art into something more personal. The lines contrast and balance in such a way that they jump out at the eyes. My work is abstract so that you can relate to it in your own way.

Sales Spree visualizes the moment of a stylish shopper fighting in the sales. It's a contradictory and sarcastic concept that balances raw violence with feminine elegance. This pair could be worn by daring ladies, as long as they can prove that their violent consumer side focuses only on shoes! Wearing this design guarantees that nobody will cut in front of you in the queue.

Be Nice
www.benice.gr

Greece

Christian Mugnai

www.mugnai.co.za

South Africa

I love shoes and I love art. I can't think of anything better than shoes with art on them. Unfortunately, so do most of my mates. So I haven't stopped since I made my first pair. I work with strong black lines, flat and vibrant colours, making the shoes very visible in urban surroundings. The baby-blue Adidas above I dedicated to my dear friend, Luca Santoniccolo, R.I.P.

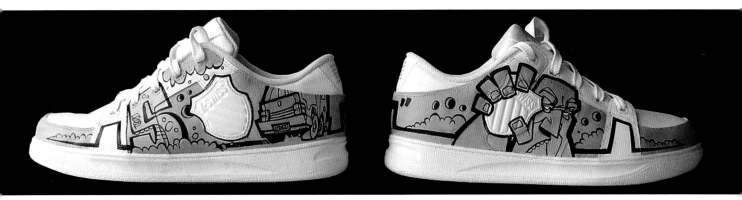

Emil Kozak
www.emilkozak.com

Spain/Denmark

This shoe was for an exhibition Lakai organized during the Bread and Butter tradeshow in Barcelona. My concept was to make shoe that looked smelly.

43

Jon Burgerman
www.jonburgerman.com

UK

I used Posca pens on both of my customs, by drawing directly on to the shoes. The idea was to create something that would look good from a distance and would hold up to closer inspection. I get a lot of emails asking where people can buy the trainers so I guess I achieved my goal.

Stephen Holding | Metalwing

www.metalwing.net

USA/Hong Kong

I have always been a fan of Reeboks since my first pair of Pumps, so when Reebok asked me to do an exclusive sneaker for their Tokyo store I jumped at the chance! The concept of the project was to let me create a sneaker that would be the truest representation of my work. It made me see my work as not being limited to a two-dimensional surface.

We're all about cramming as much as possible into the space we have to work with. It was our first shoe, so we went basic with the white slip-on and got these cheap pens called 'fabric pens'. Piece-of-crap pens, more like it, but with a little patience we got everything filled up and now we're happy.

Mulheres Barbadas
www.mulheresbarbadas.com

Brazil

Pankra Studio

www.pankrastudio.com

The Netherlands

We used black waterproof markers on a pair of white Fallen skate shoes. We like the feeling of drawing with markers; they have a nice thick, wet line and squeak when you draw. The artwork follows the stitching panels of the shoe, like a cartoon with a border. The little guys scream for help because they don't like washing machines and being yelled at.

Philipp Zurmöhle
www.phillennium.com

Germany

I always liked the dynamic paintings of Jackson Pollock. I wanted to give this Nike Huarache running shoe a powerful design. I randomly threw some black wall-paint on it, which underlines the energetic aspect of sport. Since I'm not Pollock, I wanted to include my own style, and added some aqua elements.

Louise Schiffmacher van Teylingen
www.louisevanteylingen.nl

The Netherlands

Louise is a multi-talented artist. She started in the punk and graffiti scene. Later she became a tattoo artist and opened the first female tattoo shop in Amsterdam. Besides tattooing, she also makes paintings, sculptures, photos and, for this book, incredible boots.

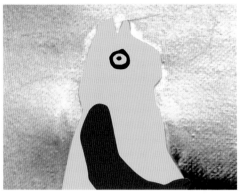

Cake

www.cakeworkshop.de

Germany

Inspired by my childhood, my creation is playful with poetic, subtle contrasts of bitter and sweet. Here, I mixed different media and storytelling elements. I used felt tips and put the shoes into a collage of paintings to let them be part of their own world. The work has no title. I chose Chucks because their material is very good to work on. And YES, I wear them!

This was for a K-SWISS competition in South Africa. I came up with the idea of an elephant man with his trunk as a spray can. I had a pair of sneakers with a cool toecap as reference. The design represents water and life, so it goes around the shoe like water into various cities.

Wesley van Eeden
www.hopeproject.co.za

South Africa

Daniele de Batté

www.danieledebatte.it

Italy

My illustrations are generally black and white and are grounded in the world of childhood fantasy. The style is naive, minimal, sometimes baroque, and always with a touch of irony. I use several tools, but my favourite is a black biro. I didn't think I would enjoy customizing a pair of shoes so much.

Michael Perry
www.midwestisbest.com

USA

A blank shoe is such a great canvas. The idea behind all of my shoes has really just been doodling like I did as a kid in high school. For these, I used Pilot V Razor Points or Faber-Castell brush markers.

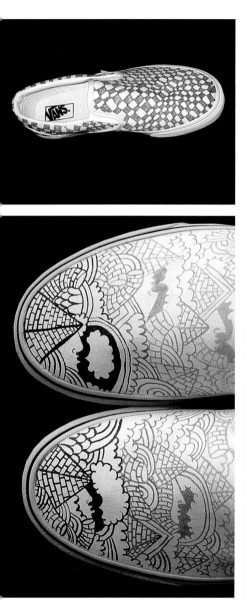

Dave White

www.davewhite.me.uk

UK

In January 2007, at the Nike show 'The Court's a Battlefield', I presented my customs entitled *The Land, Sea and Air Force*. To celebrate the 25th anniversary of the Air Force 1, I presented five key paintings, one of which was *Air Force Carrier*, and a pair of custom-designed sneakers. I was inspired by aged military hardware and the brushed effect given to metal through exposure to the elements.

I go by the name Lazy and all my work falls under the Lazything label. The brand is definitely important to me because it represents all my work. My work is generally graphical and concept-driven. It's like designing a garment rather than creating a painting. My latest work, entitled *Jail Breaker (Series I)*, is inspired by prison attire.

Tony Tay | Lazy
www.akalazy.com

Singapore

Fumi Nakamura | miniature mouse
www.miniminiaturemouse.com

USA

I like simple designs and concepts, so I chose different images for each foot and printed iron-ons on to the canvas.

This pattern, called *Onion's Glory*, is a graphic version of my character, Kid Onion. The purpose is to transform my characters to more graphical forms in order to touch more people. I used stencils, acrylic and a bit of patience to make them. This custom was designed for an exhibition in my native city.

Easy Hey | Delkographik
www.delkographik.com

France

I bought some green wellies from a charity shop with the intention of customizing them. As with lots of my ideas, I forgot about it, but finally got around to it two years later. I wanted them to have a nautical theme so I started doodling; I quite liked the pattern that was emerging so I just kept on drawing.

Kate Sutton
www.katesutton.co.uk

UK

Rubber boots have earned the reputation of being the best form of footwear one can use when it rains or when trudging through muddy pools: not a very glamorous life. This inspired me to customize my first boot. *Bootilicious* suggests fun, bright skies and a whole lot of deliciousness to back it up. I'm giving this boot a day off.

Kristel Steenbergen
www.kristelsteenbergen.nl

The Netherlands

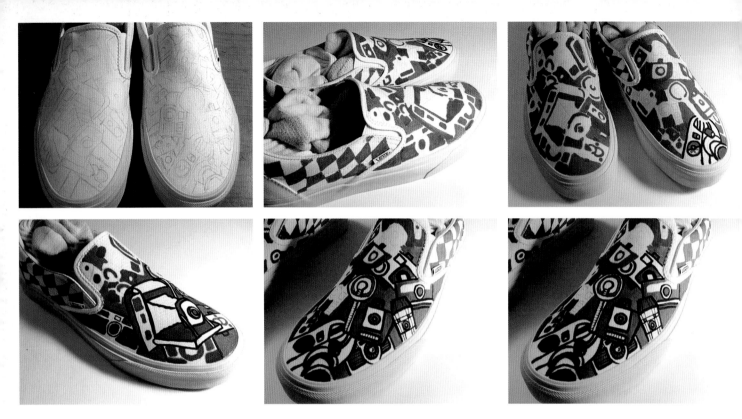

Jeremy Kennedy
www.kenedik.com

USA

The artist's ever-growing collection of cameras served as the inspiration for these *Photo Op* shoes. To him, the camera not only exists as a beautifully designed object, it also serves to capture the memories he makes around the world. He chose the classic slip-on as his first shoe canvas because Vans have been a part of his travels to and from beaches, skate parks and ski slopes for the past 17 years.

The idea for these shoes came from the London cockney rhyming slang expression 'plates of meat', meaning 'feet'. I try not to go for style, and to let the process be dictated by the concept. My hand leaves its own identity that flows through the rest of my work. I chose the classic Air Force 1, as it's a flawless shoe with simple panels and displays the custom work perfectly. The toe-box even looks like a burger bun. The skates on the opposite page were used in Madonna's video for her hit single *Music*.

Mark Ward
www.graphiknonsense.com

UK

70

James Bourne
www.ourartsite.com/bourne

UK

The clogs were produced for the *Fused* 'LTD Edition' art exhibition in Birmingham in 2007. The original design was horrible, decorated with shiny flower stickers. I sanded them down and started to doodle. I'm not sure if I'd wear them, but my girlfriend wants to use them as plant pots.

Matthew Hawkins

www.matthewhawkins.co.uk

UK

This project coincided with some research drawings I had been doing at the British Museum entitled *Daughters of the Sea God Nereus*. The images address shape, scale and form in a constantly evolving narrative. The results were a grid structure which could be applied to typography, work as a pattern, or as an image in its own right.

Llor and Dob (R) each customized Sk8-Hi Vans
and a skateboard for an exhibition of Vans and
LVL (Llor this page, Dob (R) opposite, bottom).
Strom designed the Springcourts (opposite, top)
for a limited collection of this French brand in
2007. Initially, this design was a painting and later
Springcourt printed it on their shoes. The most
important thing to Level-Art is being so precise that
the shoes don't look handmade.

Level-Art | LVL
www.level-art.com

France

The city trainers I designed were inspired by one of my cityscape images and by calculators from the 1980s, retro computers, silicon chips and circuit boards. I used materials like a black Sharpie marker and Letraset ProMarkers. I covered my designs in clear acrylic varnish for protection.

Maxwell Paternoster
www.maxwellp.co.uk

UK

The concept of *Skulls* depicts an imaginary world where everything has no personality and no identity, just a skull as a face. It was created after a short nightmare I had one night after watching some cheap horror movie.

Noper
www.noper.ro

Romania

Waste

www.wasteyourself.com

UK

Well, we are no longer virgins to customizing shoes. This was our first attempt. It is harder than it looks, mainly because of the shape you have to work with. We wanted to create a sense of movement and complexity for each shoe and treat them almost like two vehicles racing against each other on a drag strip with a typical 'waste' paint job.

Okat

www.iamokat.com

USA

Having never customized shoes before, I started with a few beers, some leftover acrylic and my own bare feet and ugly toes as inspiration.

Steven Lefcourt
www.tastypaints.com

USA

I worked as a shoe salesman for two years before becoming a full-time artist. I remember thinking about how I would improve the often ugly, popular shoes. Ironically, my first pair of customized kicks was a set of ugly feet. They don't fit and the ink won't last, but I will be doing more.

I am an architect of letterforms. I work with negative space in and around basic letterforms using black paint and ink. The first customization was for Jazz Fudge, a record label. Since then, I have customized Stan Smiths for an in-store exhibition and was asked to customize for Red Bull, Ministry Of Sound, Nike and *FHM* magazine. The materials I use are mainly black permanent marker and black spray-paint.

Remi/Rough
www.roughe.com

UK

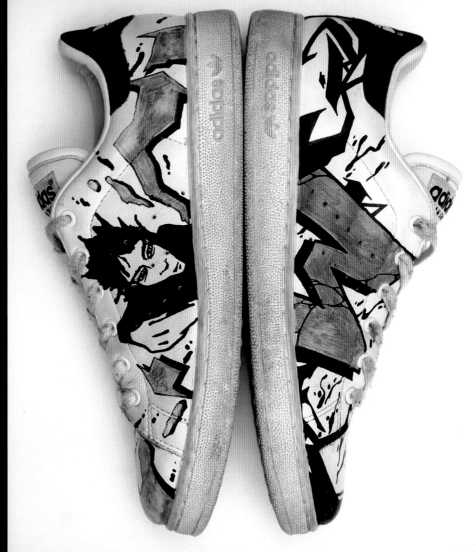

I used old school gym shoes, the kind I used to wear in kindergarten; they are comfortable and easy to customize. All I used was some textile paint and my imagination. I'm not at all into insects, but bugs are just too funny. They are my first customized shoes, but they are already screaming out for more.

Loes Jongerling
www.flickr.com/photos/_loose

The Netherlands

Acrylic paint, a box of Sharpie markers and a Saturday afternoon makes for a remodelled pair of kicks. I just randomly painted organic-looking blobs of yellow and then went back and went detail-happy with a stippling effect using a box of Sharpies to trace it all out and add some depth.

Anthony Hurd
www.anthonyhurd.com

USA

With our custom design for this book, we intended to make the most 'French-like' Nike Blazers. We used gold and brown colour, as well as textile paint and a black indelible marker pen. To obtain an old French patrimonial style, we engraved the theme of hunting and tradition.

Josh & Oktus | Delkographik
www.delkographik.com

France

Bué

www.toykyo.be

Belgium

I started to design sneakers by coincidence when a friend asked me to customize his Air Force 1s. So I designed *Heyhey and friends!* Some of my experiences include illustrating for *Juice* magazine, customizing a pair of Adidas for the editor, and recently, a pair of Tutti Fruttis for a Nike Air Force 1. The link from the street to other media is strong. I like combining these two, but my heart lies in painting on the streets.

Arjen de Jong

www.arjendejong.com

The Netherlands

Lately a 'kat' figure is taking over my dummy-books. But rather than a character, it seems to represent an idealism: Katipalism. Don't really know what it's about. But the kat chants: 'Eat, sleep, scratch!' On the sneakers, the Adidas brand is transformed to Katipalist propaganda. The geometric design is inspired by WWI battleship camouflage, called 'Dazzle painting'. It works by confusing rather than hiding.

Justin Fines | DEMO

www.demo-design.com

USA

A friend gave me a pair of Nike Air Force 1s out of the blue and asked if I'd customize them somehow. I've never owned a pair of Nikes. I'd been drawing and painting on scraps of cardboard during this period, so I simply drew on these with paint markers as if I was doodling on a blank sheet of white paper. I wish I knew where these shoes were now.

My work is a mixture of various styles. I like to use different materials and techniques. The shoe is painted with acrylic colours. The brand isn't important; I just want to have it how I like it.

Sonja Marterner
www.sonjamarterner.de

Germany

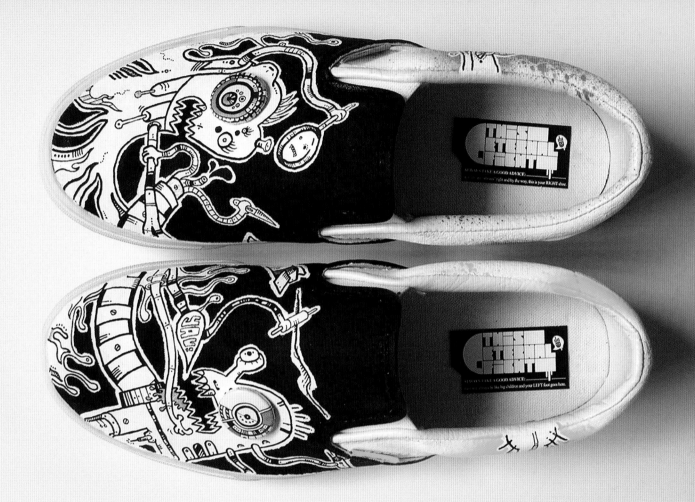

Diogo Machado | add fuel to the fire

www.addfueltothefire.com

Portugal

This Eternal Fight symbolizes the eternal fight between men and women. I customized Vans slip-ons with acrylic, permanent markers, spray-paint and gold marker. There is funny advice on the shoes, like 'women are always right' on the right shoe and 'men will always be like big children' on the left. Men and women can't live together and can't live without each other.

Max F
www.maxf.eu

Canada

This is from the 'Trash Series' collection. I make my customs exclusively with Posca pens. My customs are pieces of art for which the shoes are the bases. I work the same way as when I'm painting on a wall or a canvas.

Chris Thornley | Raid
www.sourcecreative.co.uk

UK

I use a combination of paints (any kind, it depends on the material) and markers to create the images. What fascinates me is the idea that humans are constantly at odds with nature. Most of my work focuses on the animals that are left behind.

Irana Douer
www.keepinmind.com.ar

Argentina

I used silk screening inks and a fabric marker to customize the shoes. I tried to do something similar to my artwork: start with a colour base and then draw defining lines and details on top of it.

Nick Deakin

www.nickdeakin.com

UK

On my first custom shoes, I tried to draw as I would draw and doodle in my sketchbook. I didn't plan what I would do, although once I'd finished one, I knew what I would do with the second. White high heels are synonymous with UK 'Essex girls' and I turned the volume up on this with a 1980s New Romantic twist. I used Posca pens.

Illustration, painting and graphic design are fused in a spontaneous, chaotic and strident form to rouse us from a sedate and superficial world. Textures and colours represent visual saturation in an ironic way. It is used to dazzle us; to create dreams, desires and insecurity.

Eduardo Bertone
www.bertoneeduardo.com

Spain

Karl Kwasny
www.monaux.com

Australia

Souls of Sunken Sailors is a combination of traditional nautical imagery and a neon/video game aesthetic.
Ghosts of the departed are seeping out of squids, anchors and daggers, with a sparrow flying behind to pick up
the slack.

Brandon Laskowski

www.evolved-footwear.com

USA

I wanted to try something different with a print that is frequently used. The base colour was changed to my favourite, neon green. In addition, instead of limiting the print to certain panels, I let it overlap with a stripping effect over the entire shoe. Finally, the title, *Jungle Runner*, was obvious, since bright green and shades of brown are prominent colours in any jungle.

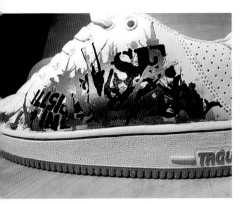

Illside Ink

www.illsideink.com

USA

With some spray-paint, paint markers and tape I covered these Roos (main picture). 'Sneaker Pimps', the touring sneaker show, displayed them. One has been sent to Hong Kong and the other is here on my shelf. Customized sneakers are a piece of art. White Tagürs, gold and other paint markers, layers of text and blowouts/splashes became my next creation featured in multiple publications and shows by Tagür (above left).

Chuck Anderson | NoPattern

www.nopattern.com

USA

This young established designer freelances under the name NoPattern. He sees his work as an extension of what he did as a kid: using his imagination to create, whether for clients or personal work. He has done commercial work for Nike, Puma and Reebok, and was invited by Tagür to customize this particular pair. He used gold pen for the detail and added the Scrabble parts and other elements.

Alberto Cerriteño

www.albertocerriteno.com

USA/Mexico

The Two Tenors, acrylic markers on abandoned shoes.

This project was the perfect excuse to bring new life to an old pair of shoes abandoned in my closet. Now they are opera singers performing wherever Luisa, my wife, takes a step. This was the first time I used a three-dimensional object as a medium for my art.

Oliver Jeffers
www.oliverjeffers.com

Northern Ireland

My shoes are stylized in the fashion of 1940s and '50s aeronautics. A bold, simple iconic customization was achieved using tempera paint covered in multiple coats of spray gloss, and stitched magpie wings. To photograph them at a major airport did not at first seem possible, so as a backup I drew a runway on a huge roll of white paper and photographed them in a studio.

DGPH Design + Visual Arts Studio
www.dgph.com.ar

Argentina

DGPH is illustration, design and experimentation. Graphic designers Martin Lowenstein and Diego Vaisberg combine art, image and animation with different forms of visual communication. These sneakers represent the way we work, trying something cute and funny, showing a different world than the crazy one in which we live.

Franx
www.sitekreator.com/franx

Canada

The title, *What's Funny?*, comes from a scene in *Goodfellas* in which Joe Pesci's character appears violently agitated when his antics are laughed at. I like to play with contradictions and opposites. In this piece, I explored the contradiction between the overt machismo (gun/phallus, smoke/ejaculation) and feminine pink flowers (inside the shoe). Similarly, I contrasted the serious nature of violence with the humour of the character being a 'joker'.

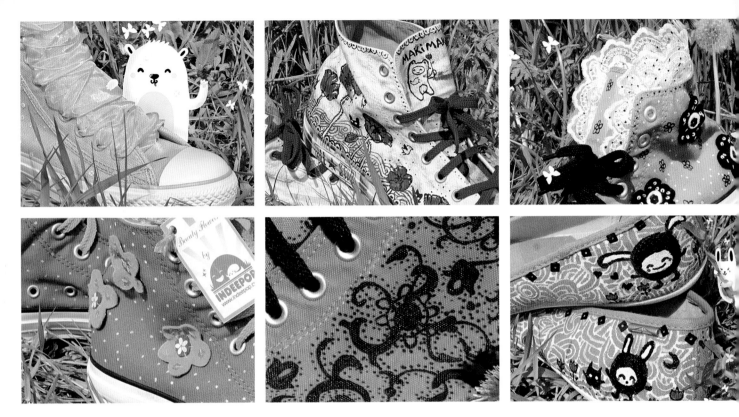

Indeepop

www.indeepop.com

Russia

As managers of Indeepop, we made a small collection for Converse called 'Converse Handmade'. Our footwear is available exclusively in Indeepop shops. We painted these models with acrylics. We strive to make positive footwear.

Astoria VIII

www.astoriaviii.com

Australia

The concept behind the *Altitude* design was loosely based on an earlier design we produced, which in turn was loosely based on the Air Jordan XX marketing campaign. Without sounding pretentious, we try to have a certain amount of elegance in our work as opposed to the common practice of simply combining as many contradicting colours as possible.

Ninja Nate | The Yummies
www.theyummies.com

USA

These designs are based on the characters The Yummies. My style is influenced by animation and ping pong. The medium is lightly sanded leather with acrylic paint. As a painter for many years, my traditional format is canvas. I did a decent amount of research before I painted my first shoes.

Jeremyville

www.jeremyville.com

Australia

Invited to be part of the Converse RED programme, Jeremyville designed a pair of Chuck Taylor high tops (above) due for release in 2008. The Adicolors (opposite) were designed for the Adicolor world tour. The pair of Chuck Taylor high tops overleaf were a collaboration with the art director at Converse, Damion Silver. Damion painted the shoes first in New York and Jeremyville completed them in Sydney.

Max-o-matic

www.maxomatic.net

Spain

Right foot? No, right-wing monsters. Left foot? No, left-wing activists (and some monsters too). These sneakers are about remembrance, context, politics, fun, thinking, polarizing irrelevant things, trying not to be too obvious, trying not to be too pretentious. My style is straightforward and basic, requiring patience and pain.

127

I have been collaborating with a hair-stylist, mixing illustration with hair. We have done some projects using plain surfaces as our support but this time we had the opportunity to work in three dimensions. Photographing this shoe was like a fashion-shoot, requiring a hair-stylist.

Valero Doval
www.valerodoval.com

UK

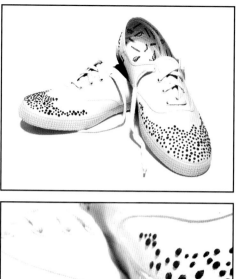

Santiago Taccetti
www.taccetti.com

Spain

The shoes are called *The Bostonian* because they slightly imitate the patterns used in legendary Bostonian shoes. These sneakers are a new Spanish classic that has come back after being forgotten by young people. I always try to make my work conceptually interesting as well as wearable.

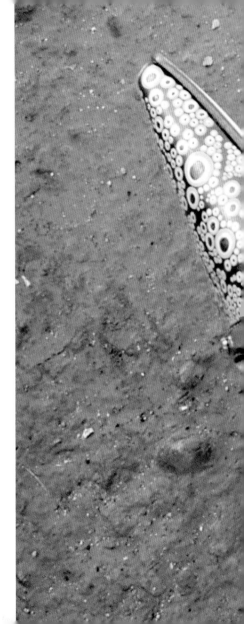

Besides paintings, I create hand-painted shoes, as well as matching bags and hats. You can purchase new shoes to make sure they fit, and I can paint those, or you can choose from an array of painted shoes that I already have in stock. All my shoes are wearable. They require only a regular shine with neutral polish and buffing. These shoes are unique pieces of art and should be treated as such!

Amelia Caruso
www.ameliacaruso.com

USA

SKWAK

www.skwak.com

France

Skwak is an illustrator from northern France. His unique graphic universe (Maniac World) is soaked, choking. His works revisit children's fairy tales and universal myths. The adventures of his characters (the Maniacs) are inspired by daily life (love stories, treason, manipulation) but are exaggerated to absurdity. They express the idea of 'too much' and of escalation through power, wealth, plastic surgery and celebrity.

Graphic Airlines
www.graphicairlines.com

Hong Kong

The above shoes are entitled *Trash City*. I used trash and unused electronic parts for this design. The bunny has a big burden on its back, reflecting the world we live in: a place full of high buildings and high technology. For *Army of X* (opposite) I used acrylic to draw on the shoe, and clay and foam for the figure inside the shoe. The figure with an x-shaped leather wristband represents the spirit of rebellion. I wanted to make the figure go through both shoes.

Tim Barnard

www.timbarnard.com

Canada

It is fun to see something I did on my Chucks, Vans and Airwalks to kill the painful hours of primary school become an art-form that is popular worldwide. The process of customizing the skates is the same one I use for canvas or 40 x 60 ft murals. First, I use a really quick pencil to get a loose composition idea. Then I use a Sharpie marker for detailing all these strange little dudes that flow out into this magical black and white fight.

Boris Hoppek

www.borishoppek.de

Germany

German graffiti artist Boris Hoppek rises to the challenge of working on every surface, including shoes. He draws with a fine line using a limited selection of colours, creating his own universe in which his main character is Bimbo. The cuddly Bimbo and lovable puppets stand in stark contrast to Hoppek's radical themes such as sexual abuse and oppression.

Richard Barnocky
www.barnocky.com

USA

My style is influenced by American folk art and modern art. Functionality guides most of my artwork. I use Elmer's acrylic paint pens and leather paint. Brands are not that important, but I mostly use Adidas.

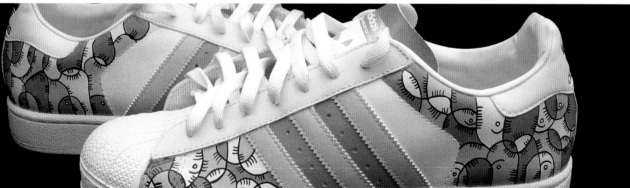

The main theme of my work is 'Graffiti Fetish' but high heels have become a significant icon in my work. They represent the fetish and obsession I have had for many years with painting graffiti. They, along with kicks, also symbolize the fetishism of consumerism in my work.

INSA
www.insaland.com

UK

James See | 1Of Customs

www.jaywhyes.com/1of/

USA

This is a pair of shoes done for the 'Meloween' event thrown by Nike to launch basketball star Anthony Carmelo's first signature shoe, the Jordan Carmelo 1.5. To capture Carmelo's energetic style of play, I made it look as though parts had been cut away to reveal the flow of energy beneath the surface. I used a Dremel tool to engrave the leather on the shoe and then added a glow-in-the-dark paint that I mixed myself.

Sekure D

www.sekured.com

Australia

I have been customizing sneakers for almost two years and they are definitely wearable if prepared and painted properly. I don't waste time working on existing patterns or themes; the majority of my work is original and inspired by graffiti. I prefer to let my sneakers do the talking for me.

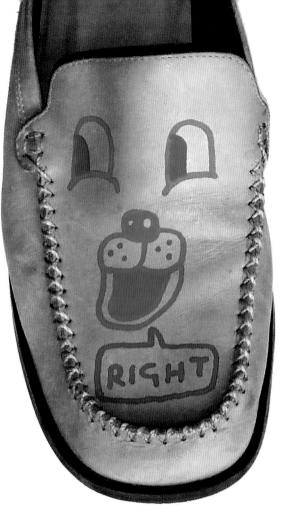

Ian Stevenson

www.ianstevenson.co.uk

UK

Ian Stevenson likes drawing and works on all kinds of blank surface that are gaping, desolate and waiting to be filled: a discarded fridge, an abandoned gas fire, rubbish bags, cardboard boxes and this pair of shoes bought from a charity shop. He drew faces on them with one of his pens.

Chum 101 & Rachael Taylor | I-Saw

www.i-saw.co.uk

UK

I-Saw is a Fashion/Art Brand. We call our custom work 'sneakouture'. The hand-engraved 'engraviti' technique beautifies the crudest form of graffiti, scratchiti. It is true to the original definitions of 'graffiti', a scratched mark; a 'branding'; a marking of hides with an identifying symbol. The brand name disguised within the *I-Saw Vine* design rebrands and reclaims the surfaces in the same way as graffiti.

These are laser-engraved sandals, footwear I often wear. The image is a 'memento mori', a reminder of death, while the text tells the viewer not to worry about such things. Any severe unease that these sandals may cause is easily removed by putting them on. Of course, though the reminder is then removed from sight, it is actually closer, literally touching the wearer.

Dan Rule
www.flickr.com/photos/danrule/

USA

The shoes were made during a series of workshops in Los Angeles as a part of the project 'Civic Matters' (www.artleak.org/civicmatters/). We did a shoes diary, producing one pair of shoes each day, illustrating our visit to L.A. We bought lots of pairs of vintage white ladies shoes as working material. This particular pair of shoes was customized with pen ink.

Hjärta Smärta
www.woo.se

Sweden

I tried to keep the concept simple. My main aim was to produce a design that wouldn't change the aspect of the shoe but add an extra flair to it. I prefer customized shoes that don't scream their difference from miles away, but if you look closer at them, make you say 'whoa, now that's nice!'

Lehel Kovács
www.kolehel.com

Hungary

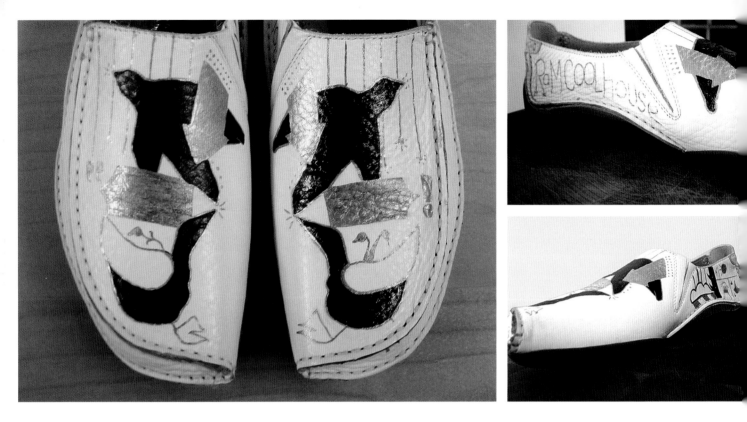

Chris Rubino

www.chrisrubino.com

USA

This pair of customized shoes was designed for United Nude. They asked a few artists to each hand-paint a pair for the opening of their New York flagship store. I worked with paint pen and marker creating images inspired by Jesse Koolhaas' music (who had also created music for the store).

Neuarmy

www.neuarmy.com

USA

The style is minimal. In addition to the gold metallic required by Tagür, I chose flat black, highlighted with a grid of gloss black dots – an element which can be found throughout my body of work. Finally, I finished with flat, black, fat laces.

I started customizing in 2005 with a pair for myself, and people noticed them. Once I posted pictures online, a business was born. I start with the customer giving me design ideas: images, logos, colours, etc. Then I sketch a design and use acrylic paints mixed with a textile medium. I have a pair of my own that I wear often, which is a great advertisement for my business.

Michael Burk
www.chooseyourshoes.net

USA

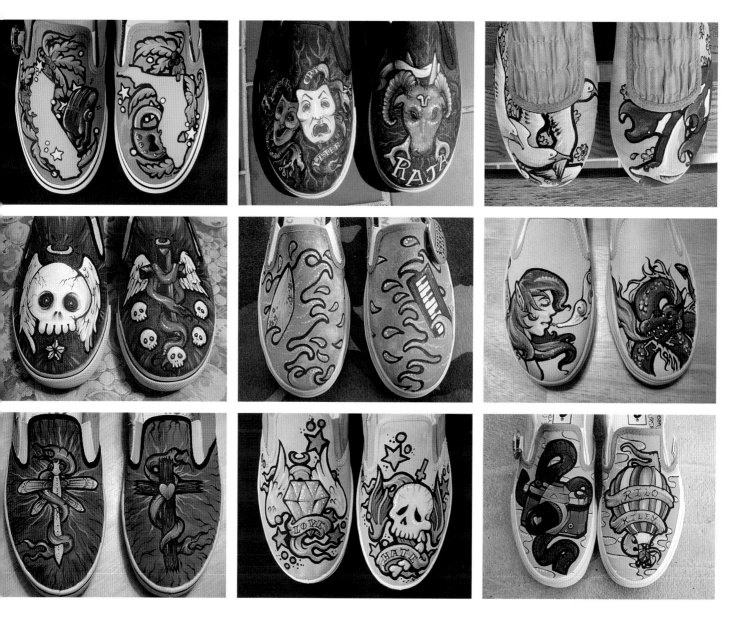

Kelly D. Williams
www.kellydwilliams.com

USA

This was a special design for the Converse RED benefit, a charity-based programme involving several artists. The base product is a traditional Chuck Taylor high top. It's a simple aesthetic; the stuff we scribbled on our shoes as kids. I didn't amend the All Star look because, for me, a custom sneaker shouldn't exaggerate. It's a shoe. Some people don't even have shoes.

Cupid Leung
www.doublewood-workshop.com

Hong Kong

I used white shoes and black markers to draw on them. Besides white shoes, I also use old shoes and include their dirty colour in the designs of my illustrations. I hand-made a doll named WOOD D, a character in my illustrations.

Heiko Windisch

www.thestateofthings.de

Germany

In April I started a series of drawings called 'Der Fallout und Wir', which revolved around post-apocalyptic landscapes and a panda-people's efforts to rebuild their world from scratch in them. When I received the assignment to customize a shoe, I got one and treated it as a canvas in three dimensions, trying to forget that it was once footwear and transforming it to fit with the concept of my series.

Marie Levesque | Missbean
www.leszillusdemissbean.com

France

I customized these shoes for my boyfriend. He liked the design I did for my handmade bags so much that he wanted to have it on his shoes. He bought the shoes and I created the first crocodile-style Stan Smith for him!

Suzuki Sunshine pumps are a visual exploration of transformation and represent the quest for awakening feminine beauty. They were created with vintage zips, vintage gumball charms, hand-folded paper cranes, chains, hand-covered buttons, lace, ink, as well as miscellaneous bits 'n' bobs.

Jessica Singh
jesskajuice.deviantart.com

Australia

164

Bondage Fighting
conanb@pclothing.co.za

South Africa

My ideas for artwork come after I've had arguments with people. I start out with two illustrations and then combine them. I try to keep an aggressive look that is sexy and classy at the same time. I am inspired by H. R. Giger and Manga comic art. I used fun, clean, bright colours with black outlines and splatters. It is important that the style of the shoe complements the artwork.

Russ Morland | LURK
russart.blogspot.com

Canada

I try to include my characters and humour in my shoes. I tend to have no idea what I'm going to paint. I mould together images of characters and phrases. I paint in acrylic, as well as using spray-paint and marker. Etnies is my brand of choice – they hook me up good. However, I have also painted on Tagür shoes.

My favourite shoes, standard white Converse All Stars, were turned into indoor slippers by cutting away the toe and heel with a sharp knife. Once that was done, I thought I might give them a full-body pimpin' and started the detailed decoration. Now I love them more than ever.

I try to find out my customers' passions and desires in order to create the same feeling in my work. I specialize in airbrush and have worked with many different media. I work mostly with acrylics and leather paints. Brands are not important as long as they add that unique touch. I have done work for many celebrities in my years and, yes, I rock my own stuff.

I call these *Cosmic Nostalgia*. I listened to the jazz artists Lonnie Liston Smith & the Cosmic Echoes while doing these. Overall, I am an artist, not a shoe painter. I do what I feel, not what I believe people will accept. I've done hundreds of kicks to date and I do them because I love artistic expression.

Kallegraphics
www.kallegraphics.com

JMartin
www.jmartindesigns.com

TTK
www.gottkgo.com

Norway

USA

USA

First, I use black ink to draw on the sneakers. Unless the owner of the sneaker requires colour, I usually work in black and white. I use various techniques; however, most often it is freehand. I love the fact that each pair of sneakers has its own story, so I ask for information so that the shoes can be personalized.

ROJO magazine asked me to contribute to their limited-edition series curated by them for Pepe Jeans. The brief from *ROJO* was: 'do it your way'. My concept was: use colours, think punk and let the drawing flow. I have used a vectorial illustration that I drew digitally. It's incredible that they were exhibited at the Design Museum in Seoul during the *ROJO* magazine retrospective.

Morrison follows the footsteps of her famous father Henk Schiffmacher. She just opened her own tattoo shop in Amsterdam. Her tattoo style, inspired by classic sailor tattoos and pin-ups, works really well on shoes too.

Man Chi Loy
www.brokenbiscuit.com

Hong Kong

Fupete
www.fupete.com

Italy

Morrison Schiffmacher
morrisonschiffmacher@artistaffairs.nl

The Netherlands

I have been customizing footwear for years without thinking about it. I've been doing this ever since I scribbled band names like Nirvana or Smashing Pumpkins all over my old, white Adidas shoes. I don't have any specific purpose or design process in mind. Possibly, I saw a picture of Kurt Cobain, with 'grunge is dead' written across one of his Stars, which set me off for this custom.

Justin Lee Williams
justinleewilliams.blogspot.com

Australia

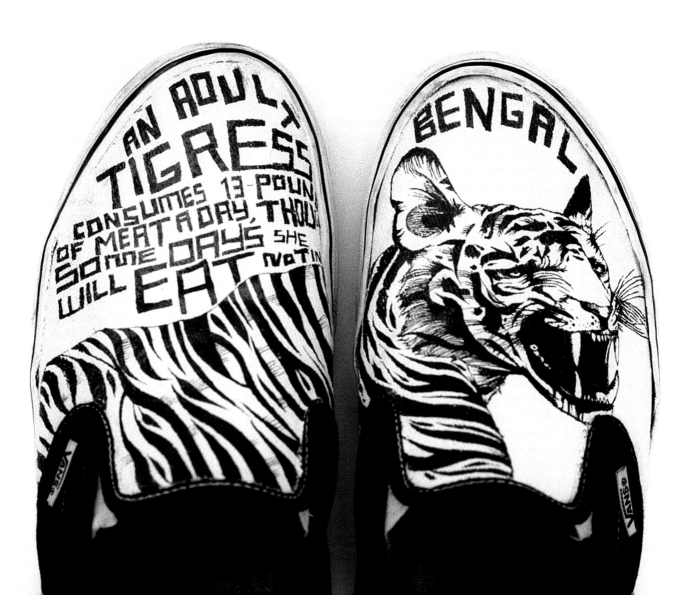

Koa

www.koadzn.com

France

I designed this on a Jordan Retro to match a T-shirt design I had done. I have used these same colours for six or seven years now. In the future, I will use other materials such as paint and pens so I will be able to wear them. These I cannot, unfortunately.

Manuel Angot | Art Force One

www.art-force-one.com

France

After a long emergence and an evolution in the street-art industry for more than ten years, Manuel Angot, a graffiti artist, now delights in customizing all things. His creations are customized through the revitalization of materials and interpretation of colours. He uses cult objects like toys, consoles and hi-tech products of street-art culture.

Sam Peeters
www.lamelos.nl

The Netherlands

The shoes are about the Fall of Man. One shoe represents Eve and the apple, while on the other Adam is opposite Satan. The material was a bit rough, so I drew on it with Posca markers to create a punky sketch.

Sonni
www.sonni.com.ar

Argentina   Being the most destroyed pair of sneakers, they died.

Feanne Mauricio

www.feanne.com

Philippines

I painted an airplane and a very interesting sky at either dawn or dusk, depending on the viewer's imagination. I chose this subject because I enjoy the idea of flight. I guess that would reveal my idealistic-dreamer tendencies. This is my first hand-painted pair of sneakers. The artwork is less intricate than what I normally do, but the free-flowing curves and abstract ornamentation still show my style.

Matt Lyon | C86

www.myspace.com/tekc

UK

My shoe designs are an extension of my artwork style, exploring fluid line-work, and pattern that often incorporates words and letterforms. I love the concept of wearable art, so along with T-shirt and badge design, working with shoes provides another creative direction. Both pairs shown here are canvas shoes and were painted with acrylic-based paint. Comparisons to 'Nu Rave' fashion are completely unintentional.

Rob Chiu & Steve Chiu | The Ronin
www.theronin.co.uk

UK

Invited as one of 50 artists to customize a pair of classic white Vans slip-ons for Espai Pupu's 'Customize Me' exhibition, we took Steve Chiu's character designs and added some old-school graffiti elements to the background using fabric and Pantone markers.

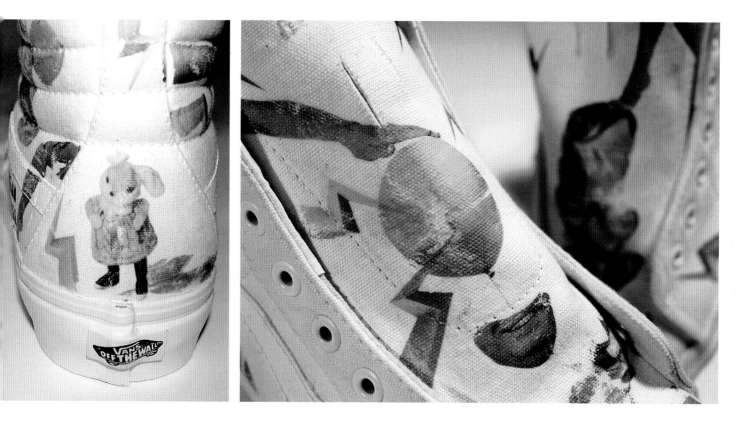

Oliver Wiegner | Ice Cream For Free
www.icecreamforfree.com

Germany

I chose Vans Sk8-Hi. I have bought this model since I was 15. My design results from impressions of the current street- and fine-art scene in Berlin and all over the world. I do loads of collage stuff and enjoy combining different techniques. I call them *The Shoes Of Flamingo Bobby*.

Taoka Kazuya creates a collage of scenes from several different moments and places. Each scene is a memory on one canvas, which is like keeping a diary.

Taoka Kazuya
www.taokakazuya.net

Japan

Steven Harrington

www.stevenharrington.com

USA

Steven Harrington customized Vans slip-on shoes for Espai Pupu's 'Customize Me' exhibition. The event displayed work by 50 artists and was organized by PUPU in collaboration with MODAFAD. His art can be termed 'contextual objectivist'; each object is part of a larger context. The object defines the context and vice versa. Discovery is the key.

Jewboy
www.jewboy.co.il

Israel

The *Jewboy* shoes were made to fulfil a request by a little kid, called Milan, to have 'new shoes with stuff'. Kids have specific wishes that companies cannot meet. This is perfect ground for customizing. The kid got everything he dreamt of: monsters, fire and dirt. The shoes have it all, including cleaning instructions!

Jayson Atienza
www.jaysonatienza.com

USA

My craft consists of combining the smooth subtlety of ink and watercolour across all canvases including apparel, handbags, and primarily vintage-style kicks. My freehand style, called 'Atienza', portrays the emotion I feel in myself and my subjects. Art is pointless unless enjoyed by all, so I take pride in wearing my designs and hope to share them with the world. I've been customizing sneakers for about three years.

When my old blue Nikes were completely worn out, I was practical: with no money in my wallet, the only way to be hip was to buy a pair of cheap white sneakers and turn them into designer shoes. Armed with the point of a dart arrow and gold, red and black textile paint, I illustrated *A few of my favorite things*, including robots, penguins, stripes and dots.

Eelke Dekker

www.eelkedekker.nl

The Netherlands

Boris Peeters

www.lamelos.nl

The Netherlands

Being a big fan of creatures and monsters, I am a comic artist with Lamelos and Kayeko. The orange Japanese monster is one of my regular characters. I usually customize shoes for myself. My favourite brand is Nike, but I rock just as easily in Adidas. I would like to see Ewings again. At festivals, I am often with the boys from Leyp, pimping people's kicks.

Danny Franzreb | Taobot
www.taobot.com

Germany

We designed these Vans classic slip-ons for the 'Customize Me' exhibition in Barcelona curated by Espai Pupu and Vans. It was meant to be a rough mix of the upcoming Bollywood style and seventies punk. We printed some complex graphics on cotton and stitched them on to the shoes.

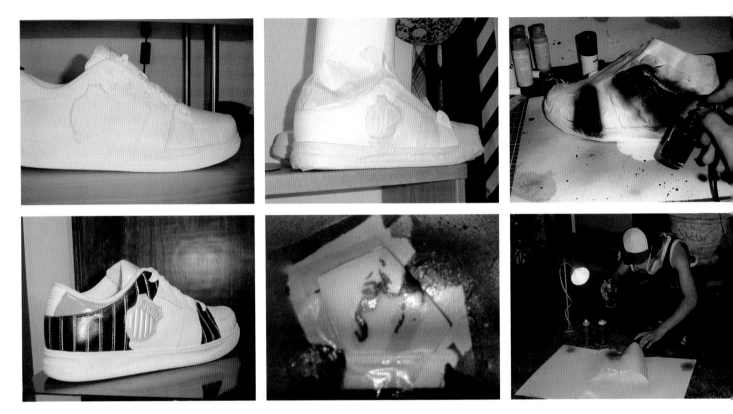

Rist One
mindgames@hotmail.com

South Africa

I incorporate a small amount of sophistication and graffiti as a key element in my work. I designed my shoes with the idea that any person could wear them, from the fashion-conscious to the skateboarder with baggy pants. My shoes were basically painted in one night as the deadline for the sneakers was in the middle of my final exams. The process involved cutting and painting a five-layer stencil.

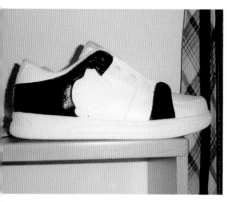

Sara Antoinette Martin

www.sara-land.net

USA

I used acrylic paint, and oil-based Sharpies on a pair of Chukka boots to create *Kicked in the Guts*. I wanted to photograph them on an actual pile of guts for maximum grossness, but under the circumstances I opted for the shiners I found in my Dad's bait freezer. I photographed them under a little bridge that goes over some marshland.

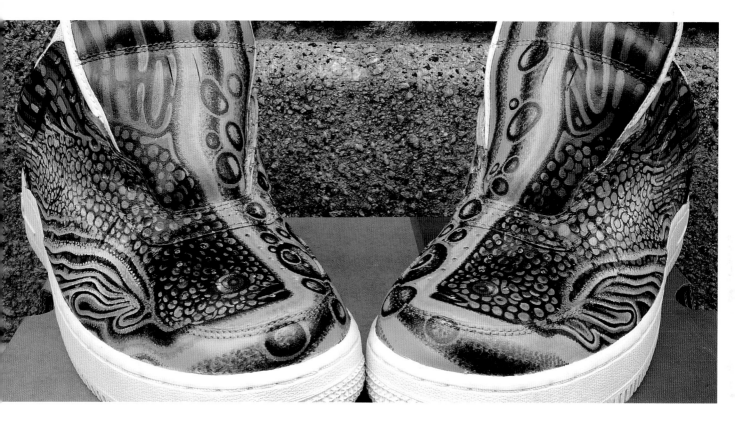

Rasheed Cornish | Tangible Thoughts
www.tangiblethoughts.com

USA

In his illustrations, Rasheed Cornish combines the best of this world with fantasy and science-fiction. He's part of Tangible Thoughts, where he customizes shoes.

Robin Treier

www.halleleven.de

Germany

Teenage Angst (left and right) pays homage to the time of carving shit into tables, doodling endlessly in school books, love-letters ending with a question mark and multiple choices. It was a time of the biggest bravery and biggest fear, when we doodled on anything and everything just to express ourselves. All that counts is the original germ of the idea, growing borderless, and the chance to reflect this. The rest is just elite gibberish.

Axel#13

www.coroflot.com/axel13

USA

Yummy (left) are a pair of white on white Nike Air Force 1s that I did at a comic-book convention. *Mad Man Kicks* (middle) were for a buddy of mine, the owner of the T-shirt company Bored at Work. The sneakers are Stan Smiths by Adidas, all white with a hint of navy blue. *Ellen's Kicks* (right) were for Ellen Degeneres. The themes of funky faces and monsters are appealing. Free styling keeps customizing fun and fresh.

Steven Bonner | Baseline

www.baselinegraphics.co.uk

UK

This was my first time doing customized shoes. I had a drawer full of Sharpies enabling simple designs with strong lines. I used a straight, one-colour style with accents so that I could add a reasonable amount of detail. The finished shoes display a pared down version of my usual drawing style, fitting the medium. Now they proudly take their place in my shoe collection!

Zeptonn

www.zeptonn.nl

The Netherlands

For *The Footicles* six bullet-tip pens containing bright ink were used. After drawing the basic outlines of the Footicle monsters with Indian ink, the colours were added and followed by darker outlines. Afterwards, the shoes were treated with spray-varnish to make them waterproof. So if you put some earth in them you could grow some pretty wicked herbs.

Zoonchez

www.zoonchez.com

Spain

I usually customize shoes for collective exhibitions, so I mainly use them as a canvas instead of to wear. I love to do it; it's fun. Being a traditional graffiti writer, the tools I use are spray and markers but I also like to play with acrylics and materials. I don't care about the brand, as long as it is white.

For my first custom footwear I had a blank pair of canvas shoes and one skinny black Sharpie marker. The most logical composition for footwear is one of symmetry, so I stuck to that. I played with negative space since I used only one colour. The subject-matter was free-ranging and whimsical.

Julia Sonmi Heglund
www.sonmisonmi.com

USA

Tim Wolff | Timrobot
www.timrobot.com

Germany

The 'little guys' are good friends of mankind. They came to us in liquid-paint-form, unborn. Their firstborns settled on sticker-paper; later they discovered shoes as their favourite places to be. On shoes they become alive. They run, kick or jump along. They have migrated from old shoes to new ones. Hopefully, they'll continue using shoes as their preferred habitat, and bring new friends with them.

Thomas Schostok | {ths}
www.ths.nu

Germany

This design was for the Converse RED benefit, a charity-based programme involving several artists. Paint and glue were applied to this shoe by hand.

Jarryd Kin | Messy Perfection
www.flickr.com/photos/jazk

South Africa

My style is quite spontaneous. It's a mess. I don't even know what I'm doing half of the time. I always prefer Converse All Stars to work on. It's the Original, simple as that.

Jeroen Funke

www.lamelos.nl

The Netherlands

I was influenced by old-fashioned psychedelia and the movie *Yellow Submarine*. Pink cookies ('roze koeken') are in there, which I would like to make my trademark. I'd customize anything, but I wear only Adidas or vintage shoes. Also, I think it's funny to replace the three Adidas stripes with something else: bananas, for instance!

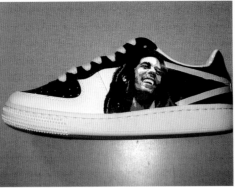

Shampoo girl – How do I look?
These shoes were customized with sand!

Sole Junkie always loved the sneaker culture, but because of his beyond modest background he couldn't afford all the great kicks when he was young. And now he makes them. He started customizing because he was challenged to. He uses his art background and influences to design and paint works of art that can be worn and redefine sneaker culture. One of his themes is painting (famous) people.

I did this shoe for my brother, Jonathan Moreno. My style is painting erotic imagery on shoes. You need to have a certain type of attitude in order to feel comfortable walking around with naked girls on your shoes. I've done customs for *Playboy* magazine, and a pair for the band Fall Out Boy.

Naoshi
www.naoshii-u-iii.com

Japan

Sole Junkie
www.solejunkie.com

USA

Kane
www.mrpussyfoot.com

USA

LouLou

www.echslectir.com

The Netherlands

These classic Adidas Stan Smiths were customized for the Sneaker Addict Sneaker Expo, showing customized sneakers and designer toys by a growing variety of designers. The exhibition travelled from city to city in Holland and had a final show in Indonesia. For these sneakers I used paint-marker, modelkit paint and wiggly eyes.

My name is Lucio Rufo. I'm a Brazilian graphic
designer and illustrator living in Copenhagen,
Denmark. This is the second time I've customized
a shoe. The first time was when I was eight years old
and my Mommy got so pissed off because they were
brand new BAMBAs (very cheap Brazilian shoe).
I had almost forgotten how fun this could be. The
title of my work is *Till death do us part*.

Lucio Rufo
www.luciorufo.com

Brazil/Denmark

The two faces of Stan are a pair of Stan Smiths that used to belong to my wife. My usual method is screen-printing but it was nice to use paint again for a change. I don't think I'll be wearing them often as I'm not sure what the right occasion would be for them – certainly not a funeral.

Andy Smith
www.asmithillustration.com

UK

214

This pair of Vans was customized for the collective
'Customize Me' exhibition, curated by Espai Pupu.
Choosing the subject was easy because we love
Japanese culture. We used a traditional Japanese
pattern for the background, a quiet little Japanese girl
and a panda character. We painted the slip-on with
gouache and used glittering beads and a red bow with
a bell as accessories.

Charuca & Silvia Portella
www.charuca.net

Spain

Leyp
www.leyp.com

The Netherlands

We use leather paint and stickers for the graphics of our designs. We prefer to use Nike Swoosh sneakers but we are open to using other brands as well. Most of our work is assignment-based ever since we won the World Champ customizing title in 2004 with the *Terminator/Terminator*. As artists we prefer to get a *carte blanche* so we can just let it flow.

MAKI

www.makimaki.nl

The Netherlands

We once customized a pair of cheap sneakers for ourselves and got addicted. Our wacky, urban, hand-drawn style works really well on three-dimensional canvases. These shoes have a blocked pattern all over, which suits the laces, and funky textlines such as 'hell on earth was created by those who believe in heaven'.

credits

photography:
p. 34: LennartB
pp. 40–41: Richard Shewry
pp. 53 and 171 (3rd image): Frank Puts
p. 73: Matt Veal
pp. 84–85: Timid
pp. 112–113: Ciaran O'Neill
pp. 114–115: Chris Heaney
pp. 128 and 10 (middle): Jon Cunningham
pp. 132–135: Romain Dessailly
pp. 144–147 and 222: Emma Slater
p. 154: Martin Nicolausson and Tom Erikson
p. 160: Amy Squires
pp. 176, 190–191 and 208–209: Nick Kailola
pp. 187 and 220: Billy Siegrist
p. 210 (1st image): Satoyuki
pp. 10 (2nd image) and 205: Stuchy
pp. 218–219: Ciska: www.cissievanderven.com

other credits:
cover art by MAKI
pp. 2–3: artwork by MAKI
p. 10 top right image: www.loganreal.com
p. 96: thanks to Adidas France and Soft Ripple
pp. 102–103: created for 'We Love Sneakers' exhibition, curated by *Staf* magazine
p. 107: supplied by KangaROOS
pp. 112–115: creative assistance: Connie Bree
p.128: Hair: Fabiano Soares
p. 131: commisioned by Kim Johnson
p. 164: splatter from www.bittbox.com/freebies
p. 175: thanks to Artmos NYC and Japan
p. 176: Adam and Eve created by God, so they say
p. 178: created for Neil Paras of NJ Sneakers
p. 180: created for *Pupu* magazine
p. 186: model: Milan Shin
p. 190: puppet sewn by Sigrid Spier
p. 198: supplied by Hall Eleven skate shop
p. 207: thanks to Nicholas Christowitz
pp. 208–209: created for the band Sneakerfreak
p. 210 (2nd image): created for Marcos and JP Boules
p. 210 (3rd image): owner, Jonathan Moreno

< *artwork by Jayson Atienza*

thanks!

First of all, thanks to all contributors for the great work you've submitted. Without you, there would be nothing but a blank book.

Thanks to Gerbrich Miedema for checking and editing the text. We really should learn how to write proper English in the future.

Thanks to Ciska van der Ven for shooting some great photos for us.

Thanks to Sam Edwards of K-Swiss South Africa and Wesley Williams of Tagür for putting us in touch with some very talented people.

Thanks to Jo Lightfoot, Susie May and everyone else at Laurence King Publishing for their support, feedback and confidence in us, and for giving us the opportunity to make this book.

< *artwork by INSA*

Miriam
Susseville.

Published in 2008 by
Laurence King Publishing Ltd
361–373 City Road
London EC1V 1LR
United Kingdom
Tel: +44 20 7841 6900
Fax: +44 20 7841 6910
email: enquiries@laurenceking.co.uk
www.laurenceking.co.uk

A catalogue record for this book is
available from the British Library.

ISBN-13: 978-1-85669-542-8

Printed in China